MW01538035

This Notebook Belongs To :

••••••••••••••••••••

Made in the USA
Las Vegas, NV
03 September 2021

29415554R10069